Heart of Yew

Heart of Yew

Poems Inspired by the Spirit of the Yew

Jehanne Mehta

with photography by Andy McGeeney
and music by Fred Hageneder

Cygnus Publications

First published in 2012
by Cygnus Publications
Unit 1, Beechwood, Llandeilo,
Carmarthenshire SA19 7HR
www.cygnus-books.co.uk

British Library Cataloguing-in-Publication Data available

ISBN 978-0-954-93269-5

Designed and typeset by Dragon Design UK

Printed and bound in the UK with vegetable inks
on paper from sustainable FSC accredited sources by
Cambrian Printers, www.cambrian-printers.co.uk

Contents

Introduction

The idea for *Heart of Yew* began in summer 1999. During a prolonged fallow period I was asked by Aonghus Gordon, founder and director of of the Ruskin Mill Further Education centres, to write a contribution towards a celebration of the yew tree, to be held at Ruskin Mill in the context of the Nailsworth Festival and millennium event, in April 2000.

Throughout the preparation period of background reading, visits to ancient yew trees and the first contacts with Andy McGeeney and his extraordinary photos, my excitement grew. Here was a subject with so many possible entry points, historical, botanical, mythical, metaphorical, that it was quite bewildering. By Christmas I had ideas but had not begun writing. The sense of urgency began to mount. Early in 2000 a poem arrived which did not even mention yew trees ('Prologue'), but I knew that this was the beginning and that concepts and phrases from here would interweave throughout what came later. I had started word and phrase gathering on my morning walks. (I call this stage 'taking down dictation from nature') and there were frequent visits to yew trees, a mere 200 years old, if that, in the local cemetery. Pages of

words accumulated and I found myself pushing through the undergrowth of disconnected phrases with increasing desperation until, suddenly, the idea for 'Nearing the Brink' emerged. At last I had the key for using the harvest I had gathered. When the poem was finished I came to the unexpected understanding that if I trusted them, waiting, listening, gathering my tools, the yew trees themselves would see to it that the task was completed and on time. And that felt real. From that moment I lost all sense of pressure and, indeed, everything came together, 'The Name of the Yew' invocation being finished only a week before the performance. During the preparation of the programme a song 'Fields of Runnymede' also arrived, based on the legend that Magna Carta was signed beneath the branches of the millennia old Ankerwyke yew, whose magnificent presence can still be seen and felt near Windsor.

In the end what became central for me as I wrote, was the extraordinary individuality of the yew trees. I became aware that they are powerful teachers and provide metaphors for the struggles we human beings encounter as we grow in consciousness and learn to know ourselves more deeply, which is so essential if we are to meet the challenges of the 21st Century. It is a gift to know that we have been accompanied (especially in Britain and Europe) by these

great tree beings, throughout our history. Having felt personally immensely privileged to work with the yew trees, I hope that this book will encourage others to make contact with the awesome presence of yew and learn from its deep store of wisdom.

The juxtaposition, during the Ruskin Mill event, of photographs and poems suggested the book, a concept which inspired both Andy and myself, but the book could not come to fruition at that time, owing to the high cost of colour printing. This year, 2012, not knowing of our original plans, Ann Napier of Cygnus Books asked me if they could publish the yew tree poems in the Cygnus imprint, so, suddenly, the whole project could become a reality and now, with digital technology, Andy's photographs can be beautifully reproduced. Ann also suggested that I record the poems, accompanied by harp music, as a CD to be inserted into the book cover. I am deeply indebted to Ann and Cygnus Books for making this project possible, to Andy McGeeney, whose enthusiasm and knowledge were an essential part of getting to know these wonderful and powerful trees, and for his superb photographs; and I am extemely grateful to Fred Hageneder (artist, harpist, book designer, and author of the definitive monograph on yew trees *Yew: A History*) for so beautifully setting the atmosphere for the poems.

Discovering the Heart of Yew

In the plant world trees alone do something remarkable: they lift dense matter up from the earth into the light. In their trunks they bring the solidity of rock and the power of the subterranean energy of the earth upwards towards the sky. Yew trees in particular show this process in the most awe inspiring way, especially those that are really ancient, for example the Compton Dundon Yew in Somerset. Yew trees can live for hundreds, even thousands of years. At times they grow very slowly, seeming to stop growing for many years, so that it is difficult to date them accurately. Standing or sitting beneath such trees puts us in touch with the ancient wisdom of the earth, known instinctively by the shamans of old, and with the depths and hidden aspects of life and of ourselves. If we quieten ourselves to listen they are profound teachers. If we are on a path of initiation into the secrets of landscape, earthlore and healing, the yew tree can become a powerful heirophant. This was the case for shaman Michael Dunning who received his strong and difficult shamanic training from and beneath a female yew tree in Scotland*. Living as they do to such a great age, yew trees have witnessed great spans of history and to

this day retain the atmosphere and indeed presence of invisible energies and beings which our ancestors could still experience. These trees still work as portals into forms of awareness which we have forgotten but need to develop once again in order to help the struggling earth. My own modest experience on this level has led me to find that a real dialogue and interaction is possible between the consciousness of the yew tree and oneself, and the sense has grown that the beings of the yew tree can also take a real interest in you. This was vividly demonstrated for me when a healer, whom I go to from time to time, suddenly asked me to think of a tree. I thought of the local yew which has become a special friend. He then said that the yew tree needed him to ask permission of it, before he could proceed with his treatment. I felt enormously privileged to discover that I have a yew tree as a guardian.

The yew is known by many as the physical version of the Tree of Life. It has enormous vitality. New trees can grow from the red fruits, called arils, on the female of the species, fertilised by the prolific pollen dispersed by the wind in the spring from the pollen sacs on the male trees, but when allowed to follow their natural inclination yew trees will send down a whole canopy of branches to the ground which root there and in time form whole groves, the sacred groves of the druids, as is now understood. The remnants

of such groves, once common throughout Britain, can still be seen, such as at Newlands Corner in Surrey. When an ancient yew tree becomes hollow, almost magically it sends down aerial roots into the hollow, which, over time, as the outer shell rots away, become the trunks of new trees, but genetically they are part of the same original tree. This process can be seen in the beginning stages in the Ankerwyke Yew near Windsor and at the stage of new trees at Ashbrittle near Exmoor.

The yew tree also has a relationship with death, not only because it is often to be found in graveyards (although the yew trees in churchyards are mostly older than the church) but because most parts of the tree are poisonous, excepting the soft outer part of the arils, which is actually made into a liqueur in Germany. The yew has been used in the past, however, for healing and in our day it has been discovered that a substance found in the bark and the leaves can be made into a drug (taxol) to treat cancer, which has the capacity to surround the cancer cells so that they are starved of nutrients.

What has drawn me to this tree particularly and aroused my wonder again and again is its individuality. Its overarching canopy is generally recognisable from a distance, but once you venture in beneath the branches no two yew trees are the same; a multiplicity

of extraordinary shapes and gestures reveals itself. Whoever is seeking to become truly themselves and to express their unique talents and gifts in their lives will find real encouragement in the remarkable individuality of the yew tree. Emerging now out of a period when it was largely forgotten and hardly noticed, this is a tree which has much to teach us in these times of crisis and change.

*cf Karen Sawyer, *Soul Companions: Conversations with Contemporary Wisdom Keepers*, O Books

The Poems

Yew tunnel at Aberglasney

Prologue

If you are afraid to fall,
everywhere is edge and
crumbling:

the puddle where the rubble of
the old road rises;

this spring about to uncoil,
all at once in ripples,
out of bole and bough;

the spleckled depths in the eyes
of friends,
when words threaten to open the
gulfs of the heart.

Nowhere is safe now;
we could tumble through anywhere,
without warning,
slipping into adjacent landscapes
we have always inhabited,
but with closed eyes,
between breaths.

Everywhere
we are threatened
with awakening.

Newlands Corner

Nearing the Brink

Every path winds away into wilderness
like wet ivy clinging to old walls...
I am nearing the brink of yew.

Rath of vertiginous shadow,
teeming with metaphor,
I cannot reach yew with words...
the phrases break off and crumble.
Everywhere is edge.

For yew I have to relinquish my deaths,
truly inhabit my heart, for
with yew, time has no measure:
it opens like a mouth.

I could fall into yew
and come up green and smiling
in the garden
before the fall;

But yew will not let me in before time.
I need first to awaken to the rhythm
of roots,
to the folded growth
always new, always stirring under my
skin,
potent and soft as berries.

I am at the brink.
Already so many of my words have
been swallowed by yew...
pages, without trace.

Wet winds, wilderness,
old walls...
The path disappears.

I want to be with yew,
at the heart of yew,
where I can hear yew singing,
that close.

Will yew open?
Will yew let me in?

The Bleeding Yews of Nevern

You look at the wound,
raw flesh, flayed crimson,
manshaped,
dripping all down from the
heart side, under the ribs;
and you know it is speaking
of yew,
but more than you:
of time, death, estrangement
unremembered roots,
earthsongs, leaking away,
lost cadences...
this thick shining blood
weeping from the trunk of a branch,
the stump of a path.

You look at the wound
and you know:
this is the way in,
this is the way through.

Borrowdale

The Great Yews of Britain

Hooded by the silence of centuries,
in the sombre needle dusk, unheeded,
the presence of yew,
beads of shadowed green
braided into the hill folded fabric of the land,
has slept a seeming sleep of familiarity;
magus in waiting,
saluted only by regiments of staggering moss clad
gravestones,
(but never taking death for an answer),
and hymned in high frequencies at sunfall
by the silkwinged bats.

Ankerwyke

But the moment is at hand:
the surface is eroding and
the old road, a freshet rising,
runs away under your feet.
You are stepping through the cracks
of your opening perception.
The wound under your heart gapes
and what you could be, but evaded,
is bleeding through
unstaunched.

Llanfeugan

The Tarlton Yew

This moment
what we could be is leading us,
walkers along the brinks of time,
hearts opening from the myopia of habit;
and trackways of soul lift and unravel,
going straight and green through spindle tall
    coppice ash,
and the shy paths of deer.

A sudden glimmering silence calls us,
an arching avenue of awe, aeons uncowled,
poised for raven flight.... and
yew, master of runes and original intention,
yew, Saturnian guardian of the sigils,
straddling the forks of time,
you erupt, in a bright splendour

of fundamental fire,
whiter than lightning,
out of the nourishing earth.

Answering life streams down in
slow swathes, sliding honey warm over
scab and welt, wound and scar,
settling into healing substance,
in fluid scripts of interlacing twig and limb,
never not being yew.

Here is the mystery,
for this yew held on:
'Death is mortal'
the song you will never finish singing.

‘Come down,
come down dark and daring,
through pillared paths where time becomes
substance of light,
into my fertile wound, time womb.
Take the waters of birth,
be regrown....
at the well of world’s beginning.’

Yew Pollen

To regrow while you die is a hardy thing:
to rejoice in the stirring bud, while giving in
to dissolving bonds, decaying paradigm,
the split and buckling bark of linear time.

In the needle dusk of yew small purses cling,
thick under every twig, gold stocks that could
replenish every heart, balance out the appalling
crumbling of the world. Down flies a bird.

Flit of feather, dipping to a branch and there...
bright puffs of pollen, dusty, shimmering,
dance into the wind, dispersing everywhere.

And look: here at this difficult door of spring,
that fullness of life which was close, shut out of the air,
is coming again in clouds, at touch of wing.

Yew at Merdon Castle

Epilogue

You are particular.

It beats too fast in your ears,
the escape you would make,
out of this place so exquisitely tight
and unopening,
your body carried unwillingly
towards apotheosis.

All night long,
your standing is unhung,
unhooking from the linear,
as you sleepwalk your heart
over stepping stones,
in the dark.

Your beating wings cannot stop fluttering
against ribs and cages,
but there is no forward but this
secondly vigil.

Can you do this decomposing,
inbetweening,
pulling you at all margins,
parchment curled, pen undipped,
flame unkindled,
suspended in desperate dichotomy?

Hiddenly, it is running on,
your tumbling life,
never once dry,
hair root, heart root
anchoring underwards through this

soft matrix you are ripening, out of
old anger and even older fears,
thickening towards earthcore.

When the rot stops
the particulate beat steadies you into new
rhythms.

Dropping through on the inside,
fearless, reforming,
funded by earth,
do you recognize this standing...
first time awake, huge,
fingers spreading to the wind...
whose boundaries are
dancing?

Pronunciation (anglicized):
Eebair, aybor, iber, ear,
Eeba, eeva, eeveh, yow,

Iure, yewar, urwen, cheece,
Eef, antiuchar, eevin, teece,
Er, aywaz, yowen, yew.

Languages:
Celtic, Old European, German, Norse,
Spanish, Old High German, Middle Dutch,
Old English,
Irish, Scots Gaelic, Welsh, Polish,
French, Irish, Breton, Czech,
Old French, Runic, Dutch, English

The Name of the Yew

Invocation

Iber, ebor, eibe, yr,
A gift of the gods is growing here.

Iva, iwa, iwe, eow,
First tree, first woman together grow.

Iur, iubhar, ywen, cis,
This tree I am, I am this.

If, an-t-iuchar, ivin, tis,
The timeless changes never cease.

Eu, eiwhaz, jeuen, yew,
Eternally and always new.

The Ankerwyke yew

The Fields of Runnymede

Where the river swings in channels wide,
Past Windsor walls in stately tide,
Where the bittern calls and the wild ducks glide
Through rush and sedge and reed,
Here lie the fields of high renown,
Where the Thames rolls by to London town
And wisdom springs in sacred ground:
The fields of Runnymede

Oh braided in like beads of green
Here islands float with the tide between,
With willows silver glistening,
By rush and sedge and reed;
And one of these a place I know,
Where those who seek deep silence go
And roots reach down to long ago
In the fields of Runnymede.

There stands a tree but more than tree
Beneath a dusky canopy,
The home of runes and mystery
By rush and sedge and reed;
And those who would true counsel seek
From far and near their journey make
To the ancient yew or Ankerwyke
In the fields of Runnymede.

To the ground where grows this hallowed tree,
Many hundred years a sanctuary,
May come no trace of treachery
By rush and sedge and reed.
'Tis a fitting place for the oath swearing
When the barons bold press John the King
To uphold the rights of all free men
In the fields of Runnymede.

So the barons of all England came,
With little trust but sure of aim,
The powers of the king to tame
By rush and sedge and reed.
There is higher law than royal will.
To the Charter John must set his seal
And to earth new seeds of freedom fell
In the fields of Runnymede.

Though islands float in the Thames no more
And ceaseless streams of traffic roar,
Yet there remains a place of awe
By rush and sedge and reed.
It is earth's healing now we seek.
From the roots of wisdom let him speak.
Oh sacred yew of Ankerwyke
In the fields of Runnymede.

Song lyric

Jehanne Mehta is a singer-songwriter and poet. She writes songs for the Earth, the Soul and the Spirit, songs of transformation, songs of hope, songs for now and for the future. As a songwriter she heralds a new troubadour tradition with a Celtic flavour.

Her poetry addresses similar themes and is deeply rooted in a love for and intimate knowledge of the South Cotswold landscape around Stroud, where she lives with her husband and musical accompanist, Rob.

Jehanne's writing is unique in the way it both traces her own inner journey and engages with the swift and immense changes she perceives taking place in the wider world at this extraordinary turning point of time, the year 2012. The call is to awaken to the heart, connect with the land and bring the light of deeper awareness to all our choices.

There are three CDs of Jehanne's songs and several collections of her poems, all available on her website. Her poems have appeared in various anthologies and magazines and she is a regular contributor to the Cygnus Review. See www.jehannemehta.com

Andy McGeeney is an ecotherapist and wildlife photographer. Around the time of the Millennium he worked intensively on a project photographing ancient yews. A series of exhibitions in the UK and Spain, articles, print sales and greetings cards celebrating the yew tree ensued. At that time he also began collaborating with others to conserve as well as explore the cultural and aesthetic responses to the yew. Andy worked on various projects with the Conservation Foundation and became a founder member of the Ancient Yew Group (www.ancient-yew.org). He has been involved in some exciting and creative endeavours with Fred and Jehanne of which this book is the latest example.

See www.andymcgeeney.com.

'My intention has been to convey both the hidden beauty of the yew and to express my awe, which the Penguin dictionary defines as: an emotion compounded of dread, veneration and wonder.'

Fred Hageneder has studied trees, in conjunction with comparative religion, cultural history, mythology and archaeology, for over three decades. He has published six books about the cultural and spiritual history and meaning of trees. His extensive volume *Yew – A History* (The History Press, Stroud 2007/2011) is the first publication on the yew tree that contains a full treatment of all aspects of the botany and ecology of this tree species.

Fred is a co-founder of the Ancient Yew Group (AYG) which has been working since 2003 to advance scientific and historical information about yew trees in order to help protect them (www.ancient-yew.org).

Fred has been composing music inspired by trees for many years. His album *The Spirit of Trees* is the first of a 'treelogy'. See www.earthheartmusic.com.

Currently, Fred is working on an introduction to the yew (Reaktion Books, London 2013), and on a tree book for children. See www.spirit-of-trees.net